THE DOCTOR'S IN: TREATING AMERICA'S GREATEST CYBERSECURITY THREAT

A Substantial Risk to Your "Life, Liberty and the Pursuit of Happiness" in the Digital Age

Alan D. Weinberger
with CJ Arlotta

Foreword by Theresa Payton and Frank Abagnale

DORRANCE
PUBLISHING CO
EST. 1920
PITTSBURGH, PENNSYLVANIA 15238

Dorrance Publishing Co
585 Alpha Drive
Pittsburgh, PA 15238
Visit our website at *www.dorrancebookstore.com*

ISBN: 978-1-6366-1343-7
eISBN: 978-1-6366-1922-4

FOREWORD

One of the most important lessons I learned as the CIO for President George W. Bush was that with all the technology at our disposal to protect attacks that could harm our government and thus our society, the human intelligence and the personal attention to detail by my staff was our greatest strength.

In the same vein, when it comes to cybersecurity for the 30 million small and medium businesses in the private sector, our first line of defense is the personal attention from Managed Service Providers (MSPs) who are trained in all cybersecurity details needed to keep these SMBs safe and secure. Working at my present firm, Fortalice, I recognize that SMBs face the same malicious attackers, ransomware, digital fraud and other threats as the largest organizations do. The fact is, cyber criminals don't distinguish between a Fortune 500 company and a small local business, a hospital, a law firm, healthcare clinics, or an educational institution.

I also saw clearly when I was in the government how pervasive foreign attacks were at our digital infrastructure. Now with years of experience in the private sector, I see the same attacks from these foreign bad actors against our private sector and Alan's book goes into great detail on these recent attacks that all experts expect to continue and grow. In my recent book, *Manipulated: Inside the Cyberwar to Hijack Elections and Distort the Truth*, I researched how these bad actors have hurt us in our recent elections to undermine our Democracy and at the same time, hurt our private sector.

If you own or work for a small or medium sized business, Alan's book should be required reading to educate you on the crucial role of today's MSP in the cybersecurity arena and why you should be turning to them for their expertise to protect your business.

Theresa Payton

Theresa is one of America's most respected authorities on Internet security, net crime, fraud mitigation and technology implementation. As White House Chief Information Officer (CIO) at the Executive Office of the President from 2006 to 2008, she administered the information technology enterprise for the President and 3,000 staff members. Payton founded Fortalice in 2008 and lends her expertise to government and the private sector organizations to help them improve their digital systems.

Alan Weinberger draws a unique and accurate comparison between medical doctors and IT MSPs and the benefits of having a "cyber healthcare professional" on your team. He brings home the importance of why MSPs should be an integral part of every company's cyber protection plan.

In *The Doctor's In: Treating America's Greatest Cybersecurity Threat*, Alan Weinberger, founder and CEO of The ASCII Group, the oldest and largest independent IT community in the world, reveals why his community of IT professionals (Managed Service Providers—MSPs), many of whom have been operating under the radar for more than thirty-five years, are today's frontline workers in the ongoing war against cybercrime and the new normal created by COVID-19. Today, in view of the pandemic of 2020 and into our foreseeable future, these companies and workers are now deemed "Essential Critical Infrastructure Workers" like nurses and doctors for healthcare, providing "essential services" by the US Cybersecurity & Infrastructure Security Agency (CISA) and by similar executive order of almost all state governors.

Alan compares how these extraordinarily knowledgeable, respectful, and thoughtful individuals perform their services to the way physicians examine patients, to diagnose, treat, and prevent disease. The parallels are easy to understand by the public, as these two service sectors are similar in many ways. Without enlisting their expertise in this ever-evolving fight with America's greatest growing cybersecurity threat, our governments, businesses, our healthcare, and democracy (it is not only about money), will undoubtedly fall victim to cybercriminals near and far.

We live in a world where data breaches are now commonplace owing to our Cloud and internet platforms, which wasn't the case thirty, fifteen, or even ten years ago. In pursuit of larger scores, hackers have traditionally targeted larger enterprises—ones with deep pockets and large amounts of data stored on their servers—but the cyber threat landscape—just like anything else in the technology industry—is quickly changing.

Instead of only targeting larger enterprises, cybercriminals are now also going after a larger, more vulnerable market—small and medium-sized businesses (SMBs). Lacking the necessary resources, many SMBs aren't fully equipped to prevent malicious software from infiltrating their systems and networks, leaving themselves and their customers open to the growing threat of cyberattacks. Fortunately, for the 30 million SMBs in the United States, there's an alternative.

Frank Abagnale

Frank is one of the world's most respected authorities on the subjects of fraud, forgery, and cybersecurity. A world-renowned consultant for more than four decades, he lectures at the FBI Academy and field offices. More than fourteen thousand financial institutions, corporations and law enforcement agencies use his fraud prevention programs. He is the author of the bestselling memoir and movie, *Catch Me If You Can.*

TABLE OF CONTENTS

CHAPTER 1

SCHEDULING THE APPOINTMENT

Over the years I've been asked many questions about the beginnings of The ASCII Group, the technology community I founded back in 1984, but one of the questions I've been asked most frequently is, "Did you know where the IT industry would be decades later?" While ASCII has grown to be a monumental success over the years, I have to answer that question, "No." I am not a "futurologist" ("futurist") by background, nor a writer in general. I am an entrepreneur who saw that if some of the smartest people in this fledgling IT industry at that time could work together, learn together, and leverage their network as a community, they would gain more collectively than by remaining siloed. ALL BOATS RISE TOGETHER.

I also recognized an immediate parallel with the evolution of the medical industry: Healthcare over a long period of time has recognized that the "independent trusted advisors," physicians practicing medicine, are the trusted source of knowledge and skills and in IT, the "independent trusted advisors" are the IT professionals, now known today as Managed Services Providers (MSPs), are the ones setting up, operating, and monitoring IT solutions.

The parallel is not just a philosophical one. There are obvious similarities between the technology and medical industries—both of which are quite arguably the two largest sectors of the world's economy today. For example, experts in both industries use the exact same words to define intrusive "worms, bugs, outbreaks, attacks," proper hygiene, and even "asymptomatic viruses." There is also a true scientific similarity why this parallel is so.

Digital technologies are based on the ANSI (American National Standards Institute) standard, which uses the ASCII code as a base (a character encoding standard for electronic communication), to make voice, data, and video transfer from one device to another. There are thousands of IT manufacturers (called vendors to those of us in the IT industry) and many hundreds of vertical uses that customers may want to use technology for. All the many small businesses, for example, have different needs, as well as home use or government or large business or even medical research labs developing new vaccines. Only an independent expert can be expected to understand or create a proper solution, or track the existing IT integrated device for the individual need. A single manufacturer cannot do this alone, since the solution requires different hardware, software, and integration services.

Similarly, in healthcare, practicing doctors can understand the genome and gene expression, with binary outcomes, the on and off switches for single gene expression (in some general sense like an ASCII code), and mutation that may cause disease, viruses, and plagues that could affect a particular individual and advocate good health regime, beyond just genetics, to make us all healthier.

In 2020, when the world stopped on account of one of the largest pandemics in all human history, the many unsung heroes—such as the hospitals, nurses, doctors' offices, and all the volunteers and working people enabling us to keep our economy and civilization going—relied on our growing backbone of the digital technology with remote communications. These new solutions are best understood and designed and monitored by local MSPs in conjunction with IT software and hardware companies. And for the first time, the federal government's Cybersecurity & Infrastructure Security Agency (CISA) and many states considered these information technical workers to be "essential critical infrastructure workers" like the nurses and doctors.

After 1994, when the internet was opened to commercial use

without restriction or charge by the US government and now in the twenty-first century, the cloud and internet is the common worldwide platform for most data transfer, the necessity of having your local IT "doctor" to set up and care for your data on a 24x7x365 basis, is crucial.

And in today's world, for reasons that this book will discuss in detail, these independent experts, called MSPs, are the true doctors of cybersecurity. They protect us all from cyberattacks, which are even more easily accomplished in times of non-intentionally created cataclysms, such as the pandemic of 2020. Personalized healthcare, called "precision health" from a genetic viewpoint, a term that is used widely not by practicing doctors, but by pundits in the medical field, is to use genetics to predict all illness or disease. Not all disease or illness is genetic. You will never be able to just take a blood test and know what your health is now. There are outside infections, toxic exposures, degenerative issues. "Precision health" is only possible with a one-to-one relationship you have with your doctor and is very similar to what MSPs do for each individual client, since each IT client has unique different needs, and the software they use is readable, writeable, hackable, bugable, and needs to be updated just like a human biology's variations and mutations may need treatment.

In some ways, the MSPs are ahead of doctors in "preventive care" since they, in effect, "sequence" all aspects of the health of all the devices and the network with the modern technology they have. In the future, humans visiting their doctors will have a more well-rounded preventive care experience. It will go beyond blood tests and EKG tests. Think about this: patients will routinely have their personal genome sequenced as a standard procedure to see a holistic view of their health.

In addition to the scientific parallels to the medical and IT industry, these two industries are moving in similar ways from a caregiving and business and device perspective as well. MSPs are paid a monthly flat fee to make sure all systems and networked devices are up and running and available to immediately cure any viruses or intrusions to the systems that may arise, intentionally or unintentionally. They have digital access to the health and care of all nodes or devices on the clients' networks. MSPs also train on good IT health management (e.g., do not click on the unknown websites)!

Similarly, the medical profession is moving to managed services in many ways as a payment method for patients. Also, the healthcare industry is working on "managed service" devices to be implanted in patients or touch screen enablement and tele-health regime to have immediate information on the health of patients in a similar fashion as the IT managed services professionals monitor all the systems or devices on the network under their control.

This book will explore the IT world that MSPs inhabit, care for, and, when necessary, cure. In these times of increasing threats to the essential digital backbone on which our health, happiness, and economy depend, it is critical for an informed populace to understand these contributions.

CHAPTER 2:

GETTING TO KNOW YOUR DOCTOR

Not many of us are familiar with the various types of physicians in our overly complex healthcare system. There are dermatologists, infectious disease doctors, cardiologists, endocrinologists, gastroenterologists—and the list goes on. We do our best to understand how the litany of physicians available to us at our fingertips can guide us through medical treatments when we're inflicted with disease. As laymen to the field of medicine, we rely on our primary care physicians (PCPs) from the onset but eventually move on to specialists when our PCPs are no longer able to help with our issues. That's when things become even more complicated as a patient in an unfamiliar environment, one where life and death decisions are often made.

Where have MSPs been? A brief history

MSPs have always been around in some form or another; they have just evolved over the years. Think about the "tech guys" you used to call when your computer went berserk. Those guys typically showed up to your office wearing a polo T-shirt and khaki pants. (Many IT technicians still sport this look today.)

Sometimes your "IT professional" years ago was a family member, usually someone younger (someone from a different generation) and who "understood" technology, even though the person you hired more than likely only knew how to do the basics. You looked elsewhere for help because you didn't want to spend time trying to fix your computer and didn't have the patience to read another one of those For Dummies books.

"It keeps freezing!"

"Why is it so slow?"

"How come the printer isn't working?"

"I didn't save the document!"

Instead of turning to a qualified expert, like you would've in any other situation, you found someone you knew who knew how to work the damn thing and work—you guessed it—free of charge.

"The whole industry, you know, has morphed again and again and again," Joe Balsarotti, president of Software To Go, a St. Louis, Missouri-based MSP told me during a conversation. "And in a lot of ways have gone back to the beginning."

Balsarotti, who has also been a member of The ASCII Group since 1991, is someone I usually check in with whenever I have a question about the history of the IT professional; he is a wealth of knowledge, and typically provides thoughtful responses to my inquiries. When I decided to add a section in this book about the history of MSPs, I knew he would be the guy to circle back with, and I was right.

After the PC came out in the early 1980s, the world began viewing IT a little bit differently. Everybody felt they needed to own hardware and software and have the brand of hardware and/or software they wanted, like a car's brand. People elected to purchase IT solutions for their homes and businesses. Remember having a "computer room" in your home? IT professionals showed up to fix broken hardware when their customers called. This is what we call the break/fix model of IT, and there are still many IT services providers using this model. Hard drive not working? Server down? You'd call your local IT technician (whomever that was at the time). There was something about owning technology that appealed to consumers—but it was not always that way. I knew then that this IT revolution would be the future, even though I did not know where it would lead. It seemed uncanny that about just 100 years from the last major human revolution, the beginning of the industrial revolution, the next big one, the IT revolution, was gaining great momentum.

"Right before the PC—and most people don't remember this—if you had a payroll or billing to do, you took it to a place to do your data processing," he said. "They probably had a little IBM or a Control Data, something, you know, with the tape wheels that turned around. They would feed the cards in or key punch it for you, and they would give you your results and you paid for the time."

Businesses at that prior time essentially paid for computer use once a month. "It was like a timeshare thing," Balsarotti explained. The idea was the business owner didn't have to own the equipment. "They owned only the data. They handed that data off to an expert, and they paid that expert for the time and expertise to achieve the goal."

Fast-forward and that is basically where we are today with the MSP model, where IT services are outsourced to a third-party provider, one, hopefully, with the knowledge and expertise necessary to oversee a business's systems and networks. And today, many times all the software and hardware may be leased or licensed to a third party or the MSP and not even owned by the client/owner of the data.

Many services—not all—are now in the cloud, which means businesses are essentially renting these solutions, but there is a catch. While some businesses today believe they can manage all their technology solutions, they simply do not have the time or resources to do so effectively and efficiently. They still need a qualified team of professionals to manage their IT solutions, protect their networks and systems from the growing number of cybersecurity threats, and assist with delivering their services to their customers. It is expensive for a business to run its own IT department, which is why many businesses don't get involved anymore in managing their own IT infrastructures.

Of course, there's more history than that, but I think that's enough for now. It's now time for you to learn more about MSPs and what they can do for businesses. The details aren't as important as the bigger picture.

That is what you really need to understand.

What should you know about MSPs

Your business cannot do everything, and it sure cannot do everything well. You are not a jack of all trades, nor should you be. While you may have several departments in your business, your main focus is always on the services you are delivering to your customers (whichever services are generating revenue for the business). For example, you may have someone in your business who handles your marketing efforts, but marketing, unless you're a marketing company, is not paying the bills; it is just one business function of many. Hiring people for business functions becomes a priority for you as you grow your business, but those costs can add up over time if you are not careful.

Sometimes a business does not have the necessary funds to add someone to its payroll. Let us use a bookkeeper as an example. Before hiring a bookkeeper, many small-business owners balance the books themselves, but they eventually get to a point where they need additional help. They may not have a background in financial services, or they are overwhelmed with other tasks, for example. When that becomes the case, a small-business owner may hire an outside vendor or consultant (a bookkeeper with other clients). Many small businesses choose to hire a bookkeeper outside of the business—it is usually cheaper—instead of adding one to the payroll, which can turn out to be pretty costly if they do not correctly determine the actual financial costs associated with this action.

At a basic level, an MSP is an outside IT firm. When you hire an MSP, it becomes your IT department—plain and simple. Whenever there is an issue with your technology, you contact your MSP for assistance, but more importantly, what many business owners do not know is an MSP is an enabler. An MSP enables you to generate more revenue by freeing you up to do what you do best instead of wasting time trying to implement new technology and determine the right solutions for your business. (Just think about how many sales pitches hit your inbox on a daily basis.) But a superior MSP—one with vast experience and expertise, and the right qualifications—does much more than just react to technology.

"A true managed service provider like ourselves is not just an IT company," Stephen Monk, CEO of Noverus Innovations, Roseville, CA, an ASCII member, told me. "It's a complement of a bunch of tools and services and automation and things in there that help them to try to think of things that we as humans haven't even thought of yet."

IT touches every part of all businesses, large and small, today, and as such, can be the catalyst for moving any such entity into new, creative directions, only possible with an IT integrated new solution. This is only possible with the MSP and the business owner working together, so she/he can understand just how the new technology will allow the business to have a new competitive advantage, not available even a year or two before.

If you want to grow your business and innovate it, view your MSP as your business partner, not strictly your external IT department. Be open and transparent with your MSP (just like you would with your doctor). Inform your partner of your hopes, dreams, and overall vision. When you do this, you put yourself, your employees and customers in a better position to handle the challenges of tomorrow, since newer technology will provide you capabilities you might not have even known existed.

Even though the term MSP is not new, it may be the first time you are hearing it. There are a few reasons for this, and it is mostly the fault of the IT community.

Who would have thought?

Why you are not familiar with MSPs

I may get some flak from my peers and ASCII's members for saying this so bluntly, but it is something that has needed to be said for a while: IT professionals over the years have done a horrific job with educating the general public—their neighbors, friends, family members—about IT services providers and the services they deliver on an ongoing basis. They are true professionals and as such, focus on the job at hand, not self-promotion, meaning they care more about solving your issues than their own (but more on that later).

Again, this is exactly what excellent doctors do. Doctors do not self-promote themselves; their peers do, many times through peer-to-peer-driven communities. A peer-to-peer referral is the best "quality" test in all complex services, as we all know.

We at The ASCII Group unfortunately can only do so much. ASCII members are, again, like your local doctor, but we have members in every state of the United States, throughout Canada and some other countries. While we advocate on behalf of MSPs every day and help them grow by offering a range of resources, and business and technical training, we as an organization alone cannot spread the word about the importance of businesses turning to experts on technology matters in a world with an increasingly complicated threat landscape. I've designed this book as guide for members of the general public concerned with how the nation's ever-growing concern about how cybersecurity matters are impacting businesses in their communities. These businesses are burdened with protecting themselves and customers from malicious actors in the business of ruining livelihoods for no reason other than flat-out greed.

Many Main Street businesses are simply clueless about MSPs and the results they deliver to their customers. These business owners— many of whom have not realized yet they are really operating technology companies in addition to the services they are already selling to their customers—are typically aware of only the very basics: They must have readily available access to tech support for when things go wrong, but that is pretty much it.

These business owners usually cannot fully conceptualize the idea of hiring an outside firm to assist with technology matters of all kinds— including email security, backup and disaster recovery, cybersecurity, and web hosting. (If any of the items I have listed are unfamiliar to you, you are not alone.) Just like a patient who has been told by a doctor time and time again about unhealthy lifestyles, these business owners only realize the error of their ways after it is too late.

While IT professionals can be held responsible for failing to get the word out about what they as MSPs can do for a business, it is not entirely their fault. They may not be the greatest of communicators, but they have improved significantly over the years. Society has essentially forced them to step outside of their comfort zones and interact with business leaders on another level. The role of IT professionals has evolved over time for the better, but many business owners who may hire an MSP, have never heard this word and aren't aware of this change in direction—until now.

IT professionals are no longer just installing software, building hardware, and responding to technology issues—fixing this and that for customers. IT professionals were able to easily hide in the shadows of the major brand manufacturers for years. But now the line between business and technology services, and IT brands is blurred. It is today a blended mix; they are not living in distinct siloes, but all part of one solution that the MSP creates, delivers and maintains. Businesses need technology first and foremost to produce better products and services for their customers. Technology has become an integral part of our personal lives, and the same can be said about businesses in all industries. Unlike the techs you are used to working with, MSP owners are business owners themselves, so they can easily understand business needs and how technology plays a role.

Without the right solutions, businesses are limited in what they can deliver to customers. Successful MSPs know how to not only resolve technical issues but help businesses with furthering strategic goals. To be able to do that, many IT professionals have had to step away from the traditional role of a technician and into a more suited title of technology organizational consultant.

Still, many IT professionals struggle with running businesses in general. Remember: They are technicians first and foremost. Their backgrounds are in technology, not sales and marketing. Forty-four percent of MSPs believe sales and marketing is their number one business pain point, according to Datto., an important software company whose technology the MSPs use to better serve their clients (2019 State of the MSP Report, Datto). While that number has decreased over the years, it is still relatively high. Reaching potential customers—communicating effectively with them—has always been a struggle for MSPs, but they are getting better at promoting themselves, especially with the help of industry peer groups, such as ASCII.

How an MSP can help you

When you are ill, you typically make it a point to see a doctor. Sure, you may not schedule an appointment with your physician right away. Depending on how you feel, you may wait a bit before picking up the phone. Of course, nobody really enjoys going to the doctor, so you try avoiding it as long as possible. If you are still not feeling so well after a couple of days, you schedule the next available with your physician, which may not be for another few days or so, so you sit around the house in agony and pain until the day of your appointment.

What I just described is how many businesses view technology today. They think they only need IT professionals when there is an issue with their networks and systems. Instead of trying to prevent problems from arising, businesses wait until something goes terribly wrong (e.g., when they are in excruciating pain and can no longer endure the prolonged suffering). If this sounds like you, I would suggest you reexamine how you react to your pain threshold. Waiting to contact an IT professional until your systems are down is not the way well-managed, profitable twenty-first century businesses operate. And it is not sustainable when you assess the data; network downtime costs can prove disastrous for any business.

System downtime costs are staggering. The average cost of IT downtime is $5,600 per minute, for large enterprises, according to Gartner, an IT research firm., that is $300,000 per hour, again for large enterprises, much less but of course, not insignificant for the SMBs. It is an unforeseen cost for many businesses and typically not affordable. Unlike just an average "cold" or a disease, IT downtime may immediately kill your business or hurt your reputation beyond repair. Plus, why throw money away on an incident an MSP may have been able to prevent in the first place? It is simply a bad business decision when you examine the numbers.

So, what does downtime mean to a business? It is simple: customers cannot access information or purchase items from you when you are down. In other words, lost revenue. For example, let us say you operate a successful ecommerce business. What would happen to your online sales if your website went down? Your sales would drop significantly, would they not? Now, let us take this scenario a step further. How many would-be customers would you lose as a result of website downtime? That is the figure to be concerned with when servers are down. The unknown is what should seriously concern you as a business owner.

If consumers cannot find what they are looking for, they go elsewhere. It does not take much to lose customers in a world where attention span is narrowing. (The human attention span has dropped to eight seconds, according to a 2015 Microsoft study.) When browsing a website, a user wants to get in and out as quickly as possible. Forty-seven percent of visitors expect a website to load in less than two seconds, and 40 percent of visitors will leave the website if the loading process takes more than three seconds, according to a report conducted by Forrester Consulting.

Now, just imagine the amount of business you would lose if consumers visited your website while it was down. Keeping your networks and systems up and running is necessary for your business to not only survive but also thrive. But what happens if your networks and systems do go down? Is it possible to recover quickly and salvage revenue before it is too late?

With the right expert in place, you can.

Recovery time—how long does it take to recover from downtime?

While IT infrastructure will go down from time to time—it is inevitable when you review the numbers—getting it back up and running in a timely manner is how businesses can limit downtime damages, especially in a world where cyberthreats are contributing to downtime at a record level. Some businesses have prepared for the ever-evolving IT threat landscape by hiring an MSP to protect them from cybersecurity threats, but not all cyberattacks are easily preventable. Cybercriminals rely on human interaction to succeed. (In fact, according to a ProofPoint study, titled "The Human Factor 2019 report," 99 percent of email attacks rely on victims taking unfortunate and improper action themselves.)

For example, ransomware attacks (which I will discuss in greater detail later in this book) are causing more downtime than ever before. Average ransomware-related downtime increased to 16.2 days, an increase of about 34 percent Q3 of 2019, according to a Coveware study published in early 2020.

Ransomware, a growing cybersecurity concern among many cybersecurity professionals, is costing businesses money by limiting their business productivity. As a result of ransomware attacks, nearly 65 percent of MSP customers have experienced a loss of business productivity themselves, while 45 percent have reported business-threatening downtime, according to a "Datto's 2019 State of the Channel Ransomware Report."

Being able to recover from a cybersecurity attack quickly is what matters to businesses. Even when an MSP does not prevent an attack, which happens quite frequently, not every attack can be thwarted, the MSP, has a better chance of helping a customer with recovering from an attack. For example, 92 percent of MSP clients with BCDR (business continuity and disaster recovery) solutions (designed to minimize the impact of disruptions on business operation) will experience significantly less downtime, according to the same Datto study. These tools, offered by numerous vendors, including Datto, which many MSPs provide in their offerings, can save businesses hundreds of thousands of dollars in the event of a cybersecurity attack, but not every business makes it out alive.

Many businesses go under after being hit by a cybersecurity attack. A sizeable percentage of small and midsized businesses (SMBs) that are hacked go out of business within six months, according to the National Cyber Security Alliance. That number is expected to grow if businesses fail to seriously consider the appropriate cybersecurity measures for their systems and networks. That is an alarming number when you sit back and think about it. Every small business owner should pay close attention to how and why cybercriminals are targeting businesses of all sizes.

Some business owners believe malicious actors only target larger organizations, but that is not the case at all; cyberattacks on SMBs are increasingly common. Sixty-seven percent of companies with fewer than 1,000 employees have experienced a cyberattack; 58 percent have been breached, according to a 2018 report, titled "2018 Keeper Report Final - Keeper Security," conducted by Ponemon Institute and sponsored by Keeper Security. The idea that cybercriminals only attack larger enterprises because there is more to gain is a common misconception among business owners. While there may be more to gain—data, money, etc.—larger organizations are typically better equipped to protect themselves from cyberthreats.

There are 30 million small businesses defined by the Small Business Association (SBA) as having under 500 employees, which includes law firms, hedge funds, medical offices, and others, and about 99.7 percent of all employers employing more than 60 million Americans or about 47.1 percent of the entire workforce in the United States. A bad actor can purchase a piece of malware for $200 on the internet to gather all private data from these individuals, such as SS numbers, birthday, addresses, and credit card account numbers.

This is what is happening today. Once cybercriminals are in, they go right into large enterprise databases after that.

Can the government help us?

The clear answer is no.

There is no scientific or political debate here. The laws, regulations, and industry regulations (such as HIPAA, FINRA, the SEC) will not make us safer from cyberattack, as even the international law of war or the United Nations will not make us and the world safer from wars.

While the majority of what the federal government is doing cannot protect us entirely, there is progress, but as with anything else in government, real change does not happen overnight. "In my opinion, the NIST 800 framework is going to become like the National Electric Code of cybersecurity which they universally accepted and recognized, but that process takes time," said Jason McNew, who is Senior Engineer at Appalachia Technologies and a former Project Manager for the White House Communications Agency. Many businesses, even, sadly, cybersecurity professionals, are not even aware of the framework's existence, so the federal government could do a better job of raising awareness around the NIST 800 framework, which, published by the National Institute of Standards and Technology, essentially provides security procedures, guidelines, and policies free of charge.

Additionally, the federal anti-trust hearings and existing action by the federal and state governments, against Google and Facebook and potential federal and state lawsuits against Amazon and Apple, and at the time of this writing, will have no effect on making us all safer from cyberattacks. Market size and possible abuses by these companies have nothing to do with the security of or the nature of the internet. Again, to use a medical analogy, your body is only as strong as its weakest link, and with the internet, the weakest link is command and control of our power, communications, financial, and transportation networks, potentially exploited not through these mega companies directly, but through the millions of SMBs, the bailiwick of the MSP.

This is in line with crime opportunity theory, which suggests that criminals typically act rationally when committing crimes, so they tend to go after targets they believe they can exploit for a big payoff without having to put too much effort in. (Remember Willie Horton's answer to why do you rob banks—"because that's where the money is.") You want to properly protect your networks and systems to deter cybercriminals from attacking you. Instead of targeting you, they move on to someone else. You can avoid being a victim by simply being prepared.

Think about it this way: If you planned to commit a crime, would you go after a target with or without a weapon? (You don't have to outrun the bear, only the next fastest camper running from the bear.)

But, truly, the best way to protect your business, employees and customers from the ever-changing IT threat landscape is to practice preventive care, and that is what an MSP does best.

Preventive care

Even though an MSP provides a variety of services, one of its top priorities is to protect clients from harm by educating them on how they can prevent internal and external cyberthreats. Ideally, the goal is not to simply fix technology issues when they arise (even though this is a large part of what an MSP does). Prevention plays a bigger role in the grand scheme of things. The overall strategy for an MSP should be to prevent issues before they arise. If this approach sounds familiar to you, it should.

There is a medical specialty recognized by the American Board of Medical Specialties (ABMS), a nonprofit organization serving the public and medical profession to improve the quality of healthcare in the United States, dedicated to disease prevention. While some physicians choose to specialize in preventative medicine, others practice it daily. This is where MSPs fit into the narrative.

To put things into perspective, let us examine the role of preventive medicine specialists. These physicians "promote health and well-being and prevent disease, disability and death," according to the American College of Preventive Medicine (ACPM). These specialists seek to stave off injuries and illnesses by educating patients on how they can live healthier lifestyles. While you probably do not see a preventive medicine specialist often, you probably do visit your primary care physician (PCP) regularly.

PCPs are typically the ones who assist patients with preventive care by promoting and encouraging healthy behaviors, including adequate exercise and sleep, and a healthy diet. These physicians are the medical experts on the frontlines of preventive healthcare. Patients turn to them first when they are not feeling well, and when they are concerned with aches and pains.

Sometimes a specialist is needed, and if that is the case, the PCP refers the patient to one, but there are times when PCPs can help patients in the long run by simply evaluating conditions and providing recommendations. If a patient is overweight, a PCP may provide weight loss suggestions or healthier eating habits. But more importantly, PCPs know their patients better than other physicians.

PCPs have more experience with their patients. Typically, the best doctors for primary care are your internists. (PCPs could also be nurses, nurse practitioners, and others helping the primary doctor who should be your internist.) Seeing your PCPs regularly (which is not always the case but let us consider the best-case scenario for the time being), there is more data available for PCPs to use when making decisions. Think about how many times you are stuck filling out your medical history when visiting new specialists. The older you get, the more tiring it is to write out all your medical procedures and conditions. (Many of us have gone through several surgeries and are taking numerous medications.) Unlike PCPs, specialists do not know you as well—that is why they ask you an array of questions when you arrive on your first day. Any new doctor you see is going to ask you a list of questions, but the point is your PCP already knows who you are, which makes it a lot easier for them to guide you in the right direction.

Your PCP is like an orchestra conductor. They don't play each instrument, aren't knowledgeable on all medical issues, but are essential to keep the music playing and in the right tune. MSPs act just like PCPs. While they provide various services, they also know their clients a lot better than IT professionals who still work under the break/fix model or are specialized in specific hardware, software, or connectivity issues. Just like PCP physicians, MSPs document what they know about their clients. Many of them use what is known as documentation software for this. By documenting properly, MSPs can quickly review what has been completed in the past (similar to a client's medical history) and what may need to be done in order to prevent future issues from arising (preventative care). Remember: just like doctors, MSPs make decisions based on what is best for you, not them.

By sticking with one MSP, one that accurately documents your IT environments, you decrease the likelihood of something of yours being overlooked. The more data your MSP is armed with, the better off you will be as a business. With the right software, your MSP can also compare your performance with the aggregated performance of other clients in its portfolio. **This is the type of competitive value a business owner could never do on their own or even with an internal IT staff.**

But here is the thing: Your MSP should not only assess, but also test.

A PCP does this when there is something else to evaluate. For example, a PCP may want a patient to get blood work done after a new medication is prescribed to ensure there are no adverse effects. Your MSP should do the same with your IT environments by testing your networks and systems to ensure everything is working correctly, especially if a vendor has new technology that, like a new drug, has not been fully tested. If your MSP does not regularly test your IT infrastructure, it is going to miss out on opportunities to not only protect but also improve your networks and systems. You can also help with prevention and maintenance by keeping your MSP informed about the ins and outs of your business.

Make your MSP aware of everything your business does, how you make money and operate, and what your customers need. When you are able to do this successfully, you essentially develop a "doctor-patient relationship" with your MSP.

Published in The Primary Care Companion for CNS Disorders, a study, titled "Impact of the Doctor-Patient Relationship," defines the term exceptionally well:

"The doctor-patient relationship has been defined as 'a consensual relationship in which the patient knowingly seeks the physician's assistance and in which the physician knowingly accepts the person as a patient.' At its core, the doctor-patient relationship represents a fiduciary relationship in which, by entering into the relationship, the physician agrees to respect the patient's autonomy, maintain confidentiality, explain treatment options, obtain informed consent, provide the highest standard of care, and commit not to abandon the patient without giving him or her adequate time to find a new doctor."

The relationship between an MSP and a client is very similar. Typically bound by what the industry calls a service-level agreement (SLA), which essentially outlines the services an MSP will provide, the relationship between an MSP and its client is one where there is an agreement between the expert and the novice, and mutual understanding sense of trust and respect.

But before you begin your search for an MSP in your area, there are some things you should know first. The most important being the following: not all MSPs are the same.

CHAPTER 3:

WHAT'S HANGING ON THE WALL?

Even though MSPs are on the frontlines protecting us from malicious threat actors from near and far; they are also being attacked from within by imposters in their own industry, and the general public at large should be aware of what that means for them—total chaos if left unchecked.

Here's the thing: it is fairly easy for anybody with a credit card to set up shop as an MSP nowadays. You do not need any real qualifications, technical or otherwise. There are no state laws or any local or federal agencies currently regulating the industry, though that may soon change. Historically, to become an MSP, all you need to do is register your business, create several offerings, pitch your services to potential customers, make a few sales, and that is it—you are now an MSP.

Of course, while this is unlikely for a variety of reasons, there is one thing in particular that the general public and business owners should take seriously. MSPs are now combatting cybercriminals daily. They are no longer simply fixing computer systems when they go down. The days of hiring so-and-so's nephew or cousin are over. Qualified and proven IT professionals are needed to confront the increasingly complex and challenging IT landscape businesses are contending with day in, day out. Just think about the COVID-19 pandemic and other threats we do not know about just yet.

Even though many businesses would like to, especially when attempting to save a buck or two in the short term, cutting spending on cybersecurity is not an option in today's world. Simply put, cyberattacks can put businesses out of business fairly quickly. The reason being is the financial impact of a cyberattack is greater than you think. Many businesses cannot afford to ignore security breaches.

Now, more than ever before, businesses deserve quality. Services must add value. There is no room for mediocrity. Businesses need qualified professionals to protect them from the ever-growing IT threat landscape. With the wrong person in charge of IT, businesses could lose everything if things go awry, which is why you want to ensure you hire a true expert with experience to manage your networks and systems, not a handyman.

The Flexner Report—and what it means for setting standards for MSPs

Everybody just assumes their doctors underwent rigorous training during medical school. Nobody asks to see a doctor's medical degree. We may once in a while ask how experienced a doctor is, especially if we are faced with a difficult decision. We scan reviews online and ask for referrals. But nobody really asks to see a doctor's resume. We just assume the individual sitting across from us is an expert.

What is fascinating about that is this: In other aspects of life, we usually make a very thorough check of someone's credentials. Before hiring a new employee, you conduct a background check, right? You also follow up on references. Need work done on the house? You ask to see a contractor's completed projects. Maybe you ask for additional credentials (e.g., whether the contractor is affiliated with any industry peer organizations or carries any suitable certifications or other credentials). You certainly do that for your lawyer, especially if a large amount of money is involved to make sure she/he is not conflicted in his representation of you or your business.

So, why do we sometimes act blindly when seeing a doctor for the first time? It is as if there is this level of respect we have for the profession. But how would you react if you found out that your doctor didn't go to medical school? Would you get up and run out of the office? Would you post negative reviews online or share your experience with your friends on social media platforms? Now, a doctor without a medical degree is a scary thought, is it not? But what if I told you that the medical professional not so long ago was not regulated?

Doctors did not always have to meet a set of standards when operating or undergoing medical training. State governments really did not regulate the medical profession before the beginning of the twentieth century. There was somewhat of a "hands-off approach" at the time. In a sense, doctors were left to their own devices, which would prove to be disastrous in some cases. (I would encourage you to look into this; you are not going to like what you find.) Even though medical training was not standardized then, it is today.

So, what happened, and where do MSPs come into the equation?

Known for being an American educator, Abraham Flexner, who founded a college-preparatory school and the Institute for Advanced Study (IAS) in Princeton, New Jersey, sought to reform medical and higher education in the United States and Canada in the early 1900s. Medical schools at the time were proprietary, so they operated like businesses, seeking profit instead of the greater good. With the desire to change the way medical schools operated, Flexner thoroughly researched his beliefs and compiled a list of recommended changes, which became known as the Flexner Report.

Published in 1910 under the aegis of The Carnegie Foundation, the Flexner Report completely revised the training of medical doctors in North America. It opposed and started the end of for-profit medical schools that were promoted by commercial interests, which were most schools of the day, and they were generally engaged in non-scientific training methods such as electrotherapy, homeopathy methods, and the like to cure illness. Medical training was henceforth to be based on the science of physiology and biochemistry.

In the early part of the last century, doctors were called quacks and charlatans by many, and there was little way of knowing the difference. Flexner wrote the following in his report: "An education in medicine involves both learning and learning how; the student cannot effectively know, unless he knows how." He went on to further state that the doctor's function is "fast becoming social and preventative, rather than individual and curative." Medical schools underwent substantive reform in the twentieth century, but in the twenty-first century, another movement for new industry standards has been taking place in the new IT industry. Members of this community, too, are on the frontlines.

In the last part of last century and the early part of this century, IT professionals were called geeks, scam artists, nerds, and worse. Before the cloud and the internet standards of today, IT professionals were mainly selling hardware, software, and possibly acting as resellers of a vendor's well-branded proprietary products—just as doctors resold proprietary drugs or therapies of manufacturers 100 years ago.

More than 100 years after the Flexner Report, MSPs are acquiring an education from vendors and elsewhere, as well as gaining a hands-on experience from the day-to-day fieldwork. They're also participating in peer groups and online forums, such as the ASCII Forum, the world's most active, independent forum, where MSP peers can communicate any time of the day about practical experience in the field about what works and what does not for their clients. The ASCII Forum is just like a private medical surgeon's forum, where only medical surgeons can talk and learn together about the minute details of how to better their skills and outcomes, without outside influences.

It is interesting how the effect of the COVID-19 pandemic changed education of all types around the world. It made online learning more mainstream at all levels of education. With regard to IT services and the work that MSPs do, the best type of education, the "know how" that the Flexner Report talked about regarding a doctor's expertise, is the "peer to peer" education all ASCII members do for each other on the world's most active independent forum for the MSPs not run or curated by a particular vendor. University education even a few years old is not relevant for the practicing MSPs, since the technology changes so rapidly and many vendors that the MSP uses to integrate with the final solution did not even exist five or ten year ago. They need instant education and feedback, the know how about what works, from their peers in ASCII throughout North America.

Additionally, MSPs have a very special duty to keep their clients' infrastructure and data safe and secure (as I previously mentioned), and proactively anticipate attacks before they arise, similarly to what the medical revolution started 110 years ago by the Flexner Report.

What should you look for when hiring an MSP?

Not all MSPs are created equal.

For instance, MSPs price their services differently. A true MSP charges you a monthly flat rate for its services; it is one of the main differences between them and IT services provider using a break/fix model. You must always compare services and pricing before hiring an MSP for your business's needs, and be sure to understand the value of what you are getting—uptime and security, guaranteed productivity, and peace of mind… not just fixing problems.

The way our healthcare system is currently set up, we pay into it in a variety of ways—premiums, out-of-pocket expenses, deductibles, etc.—which, as we all are aware, can add up pretty quickly, depending on what we need to get done, especially for the typical American. But, as expensive as healthcare costs are today, people continue to dump an exorbitant amount of money into the system to protect themselves from disease. **See, we are willing to go into debt and make sacrifices to alleviate or prevent physical pain, but we are unwilling to do the same to prevent the loss of livelihood.**

"You're willing to do anything for your body," Stephen Monk, an ASCII member, said during a conversation we had on how MSPs should price their services. "I think a lot of business owners don't look at the business as the same, right? You know, they think of it as whatever it is they do, and they forget about all the pieces that make that business able to do what it does, so they don't think about it in the same aspect until they've had some kind of disaster like a breach or ransomware. Those are the easiest to sell. Because at that point, price is no longer an issue."

Any MSP you interview should also talk to you more about your business than technology—that is something you should pay close attention to when speaking with MSPs in your area. "Tell me about your business," Joe Balsarotti, an ASCII member said when I asked him about how he pitches to prospects. "How is your business? What do you want to achieve? What are you not able to achieve? That's our kind of conversation. And we've won business before that I didn't think we were going to win because of that." To date, he's won an overwhelming number of accounts due to this approach when pitching to prospects.

As you well know, business owners want to hear about how a third-party vendor can assist with their overall business needs, and when you find an MSP that can address your business challenges with technology, that is the partner you should be willing to spend a little extra on, for you are not going to get that level of care from just anyone.

When interviewing MSPs, there are other considerations to review, many of which help with providing a framework of standards for you to follow. For instance, knowing how long an MSP has been managing systems and networks is a good place to start. Try finding an MSP with years of experience in the field and the clients to show for it. With younger MSPs, there is so much uncertainty; you do not want to put yourself at risk. Think about it this way: Even though we all know a surgery medical student eventually operates for the first time without guidance, do you want to be the one under the lights for the experience?

"Someone who just comes out of college knows today's technology," Balsarotti told me. "That's it. Well, most businesses today use three- to five-year-old technology. We all have to start out somewhere, but they can't really relate to the customer. If you're coming in from school and you've never been in business, I think it's very difficult to understand business."

Sometimes the best thing for an MSP to do is take a year to learn the business before taking on a client. "I spent the first year of our business, not taking a single client, so that I could make sure I had all the right tools in place and building those processes," Stephen Monk told me. "Because I understood that you're going to have to provide a service and an expectation. And the only way to make money and manage services is to be efficient and have as much automation as possible. I don't think some of these guys understand that."

Typically, in any business, as I previously mentioned, referrals build customer bases. Companies with formalized referral programs experience 86 percent more revenue growth over a two-year period when compared to those without a formal program, according to a 2015

Heinz Marketing study. This is same is the case for MSPs, many of them get referrals from existing customers. When you are evaluating MSPs, you should do the same (92 percent of consumers trust referrals from people they know, according to a 2012 study published by Nielsen.) It is naturally easier to evaluate an MSP if another business leader you respect is already working with it and seeing results from the relationship. "I think the best thing any business owner should do is contact the business owners they know and trust and ask them, 'What are you doing that works for you?'" Joe Balsarotti said.

When an MSP is referred to you, it is always best to do your own homework. In addition to what I have already mentioned, find out what that MSP does to ensure its employees, especially its technicians, are maintaining and refreshing essential skills. Professionals in many services and industries are required by law to undergo training to obtain certifications or licenses (barbers, bus drivers, teachers and of course, doctors and lawyers). For IT professionals, this is not necessarily the case, but there are organizations dedicated to training, testing, and certifying IT professionals.

It is now easier than ever for IT professionals to learn and grow. The COVID-19 crisis (which I will discuss in greater detail later on in this book) forced businesses, associations and institutions to innovate to meet the needs of their consumers. Considered to be one of the IT industry's top trade associations, the Computing Technology Industry Association (CompTIA), which has always issued certifications (for cybersecurity, core, infrastructure, etc.) and provided training for the IT industry, increased its online training and testing during the outbreak to ensure the needs of IT professionals were being met during a time of uncertainty. CompTIA's staff ramped up its webinars and digital outreach to deliver additional opportunities for IT professionals looking to improve their skills during the pandemic.

The Power and New Value of Community in the Twenty-first Century and ASCII's Value for the Industry

The ASCII Group, which has MSPs located in every state in the United States and throughout Canada and some foreign countries, created a special listserv (a piece of software used to run a group discussion that allows someone to post and everyone in the group see the posting and respond to it). For members to coordinate locally with each other on a crisis basis with the new special needs of COVID-19, including working with healthcare facilities on a local basis and local governments. ASCII delivered peer-to-peer content during our MSP Community Webinar Series and created a range of resources for our members during the COVID-19 pandemic. Without a doubt, ASCII took care of its members during a time in need. These efforts and initiatives benefited not only our members but also their customers.

There is absolutely no reason for an MSP in today's business environment to operate without any peer-to-peer vetting, daily continuing education on the latest threats and newer technologies, all of which The ASCII Group is a world leader. Additionally, 91 percent of employers believe IT certifications play a pivotal role in the hiring process and that IT certifications are a reliable predictor of a successful employee, according to a CompTIA study, which analyzed the data collected from more than 400 companies. The same report also found the following: IT certifications make a great first impression. If you want to ensure you're partnering with a qualified MSP, ask about its certifications upfront.

Hiring an MSP with the ASCII peer-to-peer affirmation and other qualifications is necessary to protect not only your livelihood but also your customer base. But you are not alone in your search for a qualified partner. There are millions of other businesses doing their own searches.

ASCII's value to its MSP Community is multifold: There are seventy separate programs for the members including group buying programs for better pricing with vendors, financial programs, insurance programs to allow for better pricing for cybersecurity insurance, face to face and online training events and most importantly the forum, previously discussed, whereby members learn from each other 24/7/365. Also, many times a client may have remote offices and there is a need for local IT support in different towns or cities around North America, and a member will partner with another trusted and a skilled known member for these types of missions.

In the Harvard Business Review (HBR) in January 2020, a leading article by Jeffrey Bussagag and Jono Bacon articulated why "Community" is such an important way for humans to organize themselves today especially, in the business-to-business context. "… (A) shared mission is the most motivating force a professional can feel. Communities deliver these benefits, creating a sense of shared accountability and a set of values while preserving individual autonomy." The HBR article says a true community is "…Simple, easily navigable value creation. Members can easily create new value for others in the group to consume. This contribution process is (a) crisply defined, (b) simple and intuitive, and (c) provides almost- immediate gratification. Clearly defined incentives and rewards. Quality contributions (e.g., content, support, technology, etc.) and community-centric behavior (e.g., mentoring, leadership, and growth) are acknowledged and applauded to build a sense of belonging, unity, and satisfaction. Carefully crafted accountability. There is a clearly defined, objective peer review and workflow—for example, reviewing content, code, and events. This doesn't just produce better, more diverse results, it also increases collaboration and skills development."

And even with its power to literally print money, the federal government is in the same position as you in its internal operations—struggling to mitigate risk and protect its citizens from the increasing number of cyberattacks internally and externally.

The Outbreak

When we hear the word "outbreak," we typically think about a "disease outbreak," which, according to WebMD, is "when a disease occurs in greater numbers than expected in a community or region or during a season." This popular source of health information in the US goes on to state the following: "An outbreak may occur in one community or even extend to several countries. It can last from days to years." But importantly, and you already know this: not all outbreaks are medical.

There is another definition of the word outbreak you are also probably familiar with. Merriam-Webster defines outbreak as "a sudden or violent increase in activity or currency." For example, an outbreak of violence is another type of outbreak.

Keep both definitions in mind for the remainder of this chapter; they are going to come in handy pretty quickly. The world has been changing drastically, and as a result, we are faced with ongoing battles, many of which have put us on the defensive, but it does not always have to be this way, as long as we can mitigate and monitor outbreaks in the future.

The COVID-19 crisis

Nobody could've predicted the COVID-19 outbreak.

Across the world, the virus spread, destroying communities, impacting economies, decimating businesses. Hundreds of thousands of lives were lost. Many businesses have closed their doors. Millions became unemployed. Everybody—no matter who you were at the time—felt the overwhelming impact of the COVID-19 outbreak. We knew then our lives would never be the same—and we, of course, we were right.

Governments over the course of the COVID-19 outbreak began restricting movement within their jurisdictions. For example, in New York, Governor Andrew Cuomo began issuing "work from home" mandates, eventually ordering "nonessential businesses" to keep 100 percent of their workforce at home. This presented many small-business owners with a dilemma: How can I stay in business if my employees cannot access my company's systems and networks remotely?

Unfortunately for them, employers learned the hard way about remote work during the COVID-19 outbreak. Many small-business owners were simply not prepared. They had been requiring their employees to show up to work every day, so there were no work-from-home policies in place. Many employers did not even consider what it would be like to have employees work remotely. It may seem a bit unbelievable now, but it was difficult for many small businesses (and even the largest enterprises) at the time to envision what it would be like to have employees working from home.

"How will anybody get any work done?"

"How will we hold meetings?"

"If I can't monitor the movements of my employees, how will I ever know if they're doing their work?"

Looking back, some of the initial concerns coming from the mouths of employers were fairly naïve.

But what many business owners did not realize at the time was their employees did not have the right tools to work remotely. Many employees had everything they needed at work but not at home. Not everybody had the right equipment at home to work remotely effectively and efficiently. For example, some employees did not have laptops or want to use their personal equipment for work-related tasks. Many employees could not access business phone systems to answer customer calls or make outgoing calls. Quite honestly, it was a complete mess.

Businesses across the country scrambled to get their IT infrastructures up and running as quickly as possible while struggling significantly with adapting and overcoming challenges. Even though some businesses already had agreements in place with IT services providers, many did not. This created additional obstacles for many businesses across the country. With nowhere else to turn to, many of these businesses turned to MSPs for guidance.

Unless they were specializing in industries significantly impacted by the COVID-19 outbreak (hospitality, restaurants, etc.), many MSPs saw an increase in revenue and profits. CompTIA in March 2020 issued two separate surveys to determine what specifically was driving business for MSPs during the COVID-19 pandemic—and the results were quite fascinating.

After surveying 500 professionals, the trade association found that only 20 percent of them worked from home full time prior to COVID-19; however, 72 percent already have plans to increase their investments in work remote capabilities due to the pandemic. That, of course, is good news for not only MSPs but all professionals. Now, instead of being chained to their desks, professionals at organizations committed to investing in work-from-home technology could potentially work remotely whenever they need to, giving them more opportunities, freedom, and flexibility than ever before. If we learned anything from the largest work-at-home experiment the world has ever experienced, it is that, for the most part, people truly enjoyed being able to spend more time with their families, not to mention the lack of wasted time and expense of the commute.

But, despite all the positive outcomes resulting from employees working remotely during the COVID-19 outbreak, we learned about how unprepared many companies were to operate with remote workers. Only under half (41 percent) of professionals surveyed by CompTIA said their company had strong (and secure) technical capabilities when it came to remote work.

The results of that study matched up with the findings of another CompTIA report that surveyed members of CompTIA's IT Security, Emerging Tech, and Managed Services communities as well as members of the Industry Advisory Councils, which found that 75 percent of respondents had seen an increase in business opportunities since the COVID-19 crisis. What else did the professionals surveyed reveal to CompTIA's researchers? 42 percent said they needed better support options, 41 percent had budget constraints, and 36 percent lacked the technical know-how among their workforce. This of course, is where MSPs come into the equation. To help overcome the many challenges associated with work-from-home technologies and policies, 67 percent of survey respondents said they were very likely or somewhat likely to explore third-party assistance for building remote work capabilities. In other words, the survey's respondents realized the strategic importance of MSPs.

There were also serious concerns about the country's internet infrastructure being able to handle the increase of digital traffic during the COVID-19 pandemic. With everybody trying to connect to the internet at the same time, this would surely push the limits of our country's internet backbone, some claimed. And, quite frankly, these concerns were reasonable—to an extent. What we eventually learned, though, was the internet infrastructure in our country held up pretty well to the added pressure.

"With increased traffic and population shifts to increased internet use from home, our data suggests that many users are now experiencing lower download speeds than a month ago," wrote engineers at Fastly, an edge cloud computing company, in an April 2020 blog post. "Thankfully, most of today's websites and internet applications are resilient to these reductions because they are elastic—built to adapt to network conditions and adjust their quality as needed."

Since work-from-home policies varied state by state, the company's engineers analyzed four states hit hard by the outbreak during the month of March 2020: New York, New Jersey, Michigan, and California. To make things easier, since people commuted frequently between the two states, the engineers combined New York and New Jersey into one region. They learned that internet traffic in New York and New Jersey increased by 44.6 percent during the month of March, and download speed decreased by 5.5 percent. These number changes essentially revealed that the internet was able to sustain the increase in traffic across the board. While the country's internet backbone held its own during the COVID-19 outbreak, there was more at stake than people realized—well, the majority of people.

Cybercriminals wasted no time taking advantage of the terrible pandemic by preying on people's fears and curiosities. For example, a malicious actor in February 2020 began selling a digital coronavirus infection kit that essentially used an interactive dashboard of COVID-19 infections and deaths produced by Johns Hopkins University as part of a Java-based malware deployment scheme, according to a Krebs on Security blog post published in March 2020. The seller of this malicious software even uploaded a demonstration video for potential buyers.

"Whenever there's any type of event, whether it's a natural disaster or terrorism, or in this case the pandemic, [cybercriminals are] always going to take advantage of that fear, uncertainty, and doubt in order to perpetrate crimes, confuse people, use it for social engineering purposes," Jason McNew, an ASCII member, who also worked in the White House Communications Agency (WHCA) for more than a decade, said. "They're opportunistic, for sure."

Other countries began informing their citizens of the growing number of COVID-19-related cyberattacks. Formed in 2016, the National Cyber Security Centre (NCSC), an organization dedicated to fighting cybercrime, which operates under the United Kingdom's government, warned the world of the cybercriminals exploiting the COVID-19 crisis in March 2020 by stating the following: "Techniques seen since the start of the year include bogus emails with links claiming to have important updates, which once clicked on lead to devices being infected." The following month, the NCSC took its messaging a step further by issuing a joint alert with the US Cybersecurity and Infrastructure Security Agency (CISA.).

The alert reinforced the NCSC's concerns over malicious actors exploiting COVID-19. "Their activity includes using coronavirus-themed phishing messages or malicious applications, often masquerading as trusted entities that may have been previously compromised," the alert said. And the numbers revealed later that the concerns from cybersecurity agencies were valid.

Cybercriminals attacked us when we were most vulnerable by enhancing their antics. Cybersecurity and antivirus software company Bitdefender in June 2020 found that phishing attacks (26 percent), ransomware (22 percent), social media threats/chatbots (21 percent), cyberwarfare (20 percent), Trojans (20 percent), and supply-chain attacks (19 percent), rose during the coronavirus pandemic.

Even though malicious actors targeted industries across the board during the COVID-19 pandemic, some were hit harder than others, for obvious reasons. The researchers of the same report found the following: financial services, healthcare, and the public sector were hit hardest during outbreak, followed by retail, energy, and education.

While the COVID-19 crisis made it easier for hackers to infiltrate systems and networks, another outbreak has been brewing for decades, and the COVID-19 crisis only acted as an accelerant. Cyberattacks have been on the rise, and businesses are evermore vulnerable.

The growing number of cyberattacks continues

Nobody is immune to cyberattacks—not even the United States government.

Our federal agencies have generally been successful at thwarting the staggering number of attacks from cybercriminals near and far (up by 12 percent in 2018, according to a report released by the Office of Management and Budget (OMB). Of course, there are still times when they fail, and when they do, it is up to government officials to take the appropriate actions in response to address concerns.

For example, the US Department of Defense (DOD) in February 2020 confirmed that computer systems controlled by the Defense Information Systems Agency (DISA), which provides IT and communications support to some of the most powerful people in the country, including the president, vice president, and secretary of defense, had been hacked. The data breach exposed personally identifiable information (PII), including social security numbers. Responding to the hack, DISA implemented additional security measures and provided free credit monitoring services to employees who had been impacted by the unfortunate incident.

Despite their continued efforts, US federal agencies are not doing all they possibly can to mitigate cybersecurity risks and protect their systems and networks from hackers. Titled "Federal Cybersecurity: America's Data at Risk," a June 2019 reported released by a Senate Subcommittee found the following: "Despite major data breaches like OPM [Office of Personnel Management], the federal government remains unprepared to confront the dynamic cyberthreats of today. The longstanding cyber vulnerabilities consistently highlighted by Inspectors General illustrate the federal government's failure to meet basic cybersecurity standards to protect sensitive data." Some of the vulnerabilities the investigators cited in the report—which highlighted eight federal agencies in total, including the Department of State, Department of Education, and Department of Homeland Security— include the failure to install security patches, use of legacy systems and lack of protection of PII.

Of course, in December 2020 the federal government acknowledged the largest attack perhaps ever, against our government and others in a Joint Statement by the Federal Bureau of Investigation (FBI), The Cybersecurity and Infrastructure Security Agency (CISA) and the Office of The Director of National Intelligence (DDNI). It is beyond the scope of this book to go into the details which will take many months to unravel and where this all may lead in the future.

Tasked with developing a strategic approach to defending the United States against major cyberattacks from malicious actors, the Cyberspace Solarium Commission (CSC), established in the John S. McCain National Defense Authorization Act for FY 2019, on March 11, 2020 delivered a twenty-two-page report outlining actionable suggestions for entities in the public and private sectors. Called "layered cyber deterrence," the new strategic approach to cybersecurity recommended by the study's collaborators has three layers: shape behavior, deny benefits and impose costs. While this proposed strategy of layered cyber deterrence has merit, the co-chairmen of the committee's comments at the beginning of the report should not be ignored.

Attributed to both Senator Angus King and Representative Mike Gallagher, the chairman's letter, which conceptualizes the report's overall findings, also highlighted the state of cybersecurity at the time. The co-chairmen, both of whom encouraged the readers of their report to demand more from the federal government and private sector when it comes to cybersecurity precautions, sadly, painted a gloomy outlook for the country if it did not take drastic measures:

"The reality is that we are dangerously insecure in cyber. Your entire life—your paycheck, your healthcare, your electricity—increasingly relies on networks of digital devices that store, process, and analyze data. These networks are vulnerable, if not already compromised. Our country has lost hundreds of billions of dollars to nation-state-sponsored intellectual property theft due to cyber espionage. A major cyberattack on the nation's critical infrastructure and economic system would create chaos and lasting damage exceeding that wreaked by fires in California, floods in the Midwest, and hurricanes in the Southeast."

Even though mainstream media outlets continue to report on the ever-growing number of cyberattacks, we quickly forget about many of these incidents—many significant ones too. Remember when a suspected Vietnamese state-sponsored hacking group attacked BMW and Hyundai networks in December 2019? What about when state-sponsored Chinese hackers in July 2019 conducted a spear-phishing campaign against employees of three major utility companies in the US? How about when pharmaceutical giant Bayer in April 2019 revealed it had prevented an attack by Chinese hackers targeting sensitive intellectual property? Did you forget about when US agencies in October 2019 warned President Trump that China and Russia eavesdropped on phone calls he unfortunately made from an unsecured line? Fortunately, for us, there are currently institutions keeping track of major cyber incidents across the world.

For instance, founded in 1962, The Center for Strategic and International Studies (CSIS), a think tank based in Washington, DC, keeps a running list of major cyber incidents targeting "government agencies, defense, and high-tech companies, or economic crimes with losses of more than a million dollars." The list, which CSIS updates whenever it receives information on a significant cyber incident, goes all the way back to 2006.

Dated May 2006, the first entry on the list reads as follows: "The Department of State's networks were hacked, and unknown foreign intruders downloaded terabytes of information. If Chinese or Russian spies had backed a truck up to the State Department, smashed the glass doors, tied up the guards, and spent the night carting off file cabinets, it would constitute an act of war. But when it happens in cyberspace, we barely notice." Look at our "political" world today and see if we could ever agree on what the Russians did and why, when, and how? The fear of foreign influence and attacks on our "life, liberty, and pursuit of happiness" was prominently noted even by George Washington in 1796 in his farewell address to our nation, where he said, "the jealousy of a free people ought to be constantly awake, since history and experience prove that foreign influence is one of the most baneful foes of republican government."

If cybercriminals can successfully infiltrate the systems and networks of one of the most powerful governments in the world, what are they capable of doing to the 30 million small businesses in the United States alone?

It is important to note the following: hackers are oftentimes opportunists, as Jason McNew, an ASCII Group member, noted earlier, waiting for the right moment to carry out their attacks—are just like infectious virus agents. As you know, your immune system is designed to protect you from infectious agents—viruses, bacteria, fungi, etc.— but when it is weakened—from alcohol, disease, poor nutrition, smoking, etc.—these infectious agents have higher chances of successfully invading your internal defense mechanisms, which is one of the reasons why physicians are always trying to get us to choose healthier lifestyles. When you take care of the basics, essentially practicing healthy habits, the likelihood of you contracting something decreases. The same can be said about your IT systems and networks and networked devices.

Even though many small business owners are aware of the threat cybercriminals pose to their livelihoods, they are not taking the proper actions to protect themselves. The National Cyber Security Alliance (NCSA), an organization dedicated to promoting cybersecurity and privacy education, and awareness, polled more than 1,000 small-business decision-makers in the US in 2019 about how they're responding to the growing number cybersecurity threats. 88 percent of the survey's respondents said they believed they were being targeted by cybercriminals. Considering the available data on the topic, their concerns were justified; despite this, only 58 percent said they had response plans they could immediately put into action when cybercriminals infiltrated their systems. Think about that for a moment. Imagine a doctor informing you that they were going to wing it after diagnosing you with serious—potentially fatal—illnesses (like heart disease, for instance) instead of putting treatment plans immediately into motion. Would you be okay with that? I certainly would not be. In fact, many of these patients would go elsewhere for additional medical opinions for treatments.

Businesses of all sizes must do a better job of properly securing their systems and networks. Cybercriminals are relentless and will stop at nothing. And when you examine the data, you will quickly realize that *all* businesses in the US need the help of MSPs sooner rather than later.

US organizations have reported the compromise of more than five billion records in 2019, according to the ForgeRock 2020 Consumer Identity Breach Report. The numbers are not expected to dip anytime soon.

With the help of the frontline workers the MSPs, businesses can better protect themselves from the ever-evolving IT threat landscape. But if businesses wait too late to act, they will not be able to effectively and efficiently protect their systems and networks from the growing number of cyberattacks in the current business climate.

CHAPTER 4:

The Future of Work and Medicine

Even though there is a lot that can be said about the future of the increasingly complex cyber threat landscape—especially after the worldwide outbreak of COVID-19 and the destruction committed by malicious actors throughout the crisis—but one thing is certain: MSPs, fortunately for us, are not going anywhere. While that is a positive outlook for MSPs, it is a bleak prediction for businesses.

The "new normal"

Many businesses more than likely will accept what has been coined as the "new normal" by many, meaning business leaders are less likely to resist the urge to tell their employees they cannot work from home. Instead, many businesses will adopt new work-from-home policies and encourage flexible work schedules as a result. Facebook, Twitter, Apple, Amazon and other tech giants modified their work-from-home policies amid the COVID-19 pandemic, allowing their employees to continue to work remotely after the outbreak subsides.

Of course, working from home is a large component of the new normal. 42 percent of employees have been working from home as a result of the COVID-19 pandemic, according to a PC Matic report, titled "COVID-19: Work from Home Trends," published in May 2020.

The largest work-from-home experiment our nation has ever conducted is expected to continue and become more widespread even after the coronavirus crisis subsides.

Nearly 30 percent of the US workforce will be working-from-home multiple days a week by the end of 2021, according to a study by Global Workplace Analytics (GWA), a research and consulting firm. Of course, this is all good news for employees, especially millennials, with an overwhelming number of them looking to work from home (92 percent, according to 2013 study conducted by Upwork, known at the time as oDesk). While younger generations may have been the ones originally pushing to work from home, the additional flexibility and freedom during the workday is alluring to workers of all ages.

Many employees will take advantage of being able to work remotely, which, of course, has its pros and cons just like anything else in this world. But while this new normal opens many opportunities for employees, especially those who may not want to live where their companies operate or endure lengthy commutes, it puts businesses at risk if they do not adhere to proper cybersecurity precautions moving forward.

For instance, many employees working from home aren't taking cybersecurity concerns seriously, even with cybersecurity attacks on the rise. More than half (52 percent) of employees feel they can get away with riskier behavior when working remotely, according to a May 2020 report, titled "The State of Data Loss Prevention 2020," released by researchers at cybersecurity company Tessian.

Some of the top reasons why employees are less likely to follow safe data practices when working remotely include not working on their usual devices and being distracted, according to the same report. "Most of us can relate," the researchers noted. "When working remotely—especially from home—people have other responsibilities or distractions like childcare and roommates, and more often than not, they don't have dedicated workstations like they do in their normal office environment. This isn't trivial." As valid as these reasons may be, they do not make it any easier for organizations to protect themselves from cyberattacks.

Many employers failed to properly protect their employees working remotely during the COVID-19 pandemic. For example, 93 percent of employees did not receive advanced business antivirus software to install on their personal devices from their employers, according to the previously cited PC Matic report.

By failing to provide their employees with these more secure essentials, many businesses quickly realized the importance of outsourcing IT to the professionals. Unfortunately for them, the cybersecurity skills gap became apparent.

Closing the cybersecurity skills gap should be one of our nation's top priorities

Even with MSPs coming to our rescue, closing the cybersecurity skills gap must be a top priority for us as a nation. The worldwide IT security skills shortage is a problem we as a country must take responsibility for if we want to be able to properly protect ourselves from the increasing number of cyberattacks over the longer term.

The global cybersecurity workforce shortage has been projected to reach upwards of 1.8 million unfilled positions by 2022, according to a 2017 Frost & Sullivan study on the subject. We are in dire need of more qualified, skilled, and professionally trained technical experts who not only know how to properly secure IT infrastructures but can also keep up with the increasing number of hackers who are sophisticated enough to be constantly innovating and scheming of new ways to harm our institutions.

For instance, cybercriminals are continuing to deploy ransomware attacks on entities designed to not only keep us safe but healthy and educated. The numbers are staggering: Ransomware attacks impacted nearly 1,000 government agencies, educational establishments and healthcare providers in 2019, according to an Emsisoft study published in December 2019. In addition to causing financial damage (more than $7.5 billion worth), these cyber incidents unfortunately disrupted these institutions operationally, which put countless lives at risk by interrupting 911 services, holding medical records hostage, etc.

Of course, these hackers succeeded in their efforts due to a variety of reasons; however, the report's authors mainly attributed the increase in ransomware attacks to various organizations' existing security weaknesses, as well as the development of increasingly sophisticated attack mechanisms specifically designed to exploit them. Combined, these factors created a near-perfect storm. The need for cybersecurity specialists has never been greater.

Another study revealed the following: 82 percent of employers have a shortage of cybersecurity skills; 71 percent believe this shortage causes direct and measurable damage to their organizations. The study—published by Center for Strategic and International Studies (CSIS) in January 2019, IT decision-makers across eight countries—highlights several recommendations, one of which is worth noting: "Companies should build relationships with local educators to communicate critical workforce needs and skills gaps. Improved communication between employers and learning institutions will help align the cybersecurity talent pipeline with the needs of industry." The cybersecurity skills gap, which has been a growing concern for several years, is impacting every business, and it is preventing MSPs from properly protecting their customers when their customers need them the most.

Even though the IT community has been shifting more and more of its efforts toward cybersecurity, they can do better. There are 2.8 million cybersecurity professionals worldwide, according to a Cybersecurity Workforce Study from (ISC)². While IT professionals are aware of the growing need for cybersecurity professionals, their efforts have gone unnoticed.

Let us go back to comparing MSPs to physicians for a moment. You see a doctor when you are feeling ill, but what if a doctor is not available? Yes, physicians are busy, and their schedules fill up quickly; however, how long should you have to wait to see a doctor? Would it not make sense for the doctor's office you visit to hire another doctor if there is demand? Of course, it would! They would probably agree with you, but what if there were not any doctors looking for work? Your doctor's office may not be able to get to you in a timely manner, which is a problem if your body is under attack by foreign invader germs (bacteria, viruses, parasites). The same is true for businesses in need of protection from cybersecurity threats.

Finding cybersecurity professionals is a top challenge for many MSPs. Forty percent of MSPs cannot obtain and retain the skills necessary to deliver cybersecurity services effectively to their customers, according to a 2019 report published by Continuum, an IT management software provider for MSPs. While you may think this workforce shortage only negatively impacts MSPs, think again. Because of this challenge, which is not expected to abate anytime soon, especially after the COVID-19 pandemic, 67 percent of MSPs do not feel fully confident in their ability to defend their clients against cyberattacks, the same study revealed. Now, that sounds like a data point a business owner should be worried about, does it not? What if the doctor's office felt the same way about its ability to provide care to you? Would you want to go to that office? If the majority of doctors' offices felt the same way, where would you go for care? Would you forgo it? Put your body at risk for potential health complications in the future?

Business leaders are also recognizing the shortage of cybersecurity skills at their companies. 76 percent of business executives are seeing this, according to research published in 2020 by Stott and May, a technology recruitment firm. When business leaders cannot find talent they need, they look elsewhere, turning to outside businesses for assistance.

But if you think you are in the clear because you are not a business owner, think again. There is more at stake than you may realize. The cybersecurity skills shortage is an issue we are all going to be aware of soon enough if we fail to act swiftly. Our not-so-distant future is about to get more complicated—and if we do not act immediately, MSPs are not going to be able to properly protect our communities—many of which are more connected than ever before when you consider the growing number of connected devices in major cities across the country—from outside intruders looking to cause harm to friends, family members, and neighbors.

How "smart" are smart cities?

Cybercriminals are paying close attention to governments investing in the development of smart cities. "A smart city is a complex ecosystem of municipal services, public and private entities, people, processes, devices, and city infrastructure that constantly interact with each other," according to Deloitte, the major financial and consulting firm. These urban developments are connected by underlying technologies—including sensors, robotics, and the internet of things (IoT)—and gaining the attention of malicious actors.

Hackers have taken a keen interest in smart cities for their growth potential. Worldwide spending on smart cities initiatives will reach $189.5 billion in 2023, according to an IDC report in June 2019. The researchers of the same report discovered the following: The United States, Western Europe, and China will account for more than 70 percent of all smart cities spending throughout the forecast. "Regional and municipal governments are working hard to keep pace with technology advances and take advantage of new opportunities in the context of risk management, public expectations, and funding needs to scale initiatives," said Ruthbea Yesner, vice president of IDC Government Insights and Smart Cities and Communities. "Many are moving to incorporate Smart City use cases into budgets, or financing efforts through more traditional means. This is helping to grow investments." There will be at least twenty-six full-fledged major smart cities worldwide by 2025, according to market research company Frost and Sullivan. While many municipalities are turning to smart city technologies for solutions, cybercriminals are scheming behind the scenes.

With technology constantly evolving, securing smart cities is no easy feat for municipalities. Staying up to date on security trends is what sets back many cybersecurity professionals; the threat environment is constantly changing. Ahead of the experts, cybercriminals easily outmaneuver security measures when they are not properly implemented. Ensuring networks, systems, and devices are correctly configured is key to limiting the number of cyberattacks on smart cities, but mistakes are sometimes made.

Now, while you do not necessarily need to know the technical details behind why smart cities are so vulnerable to cyberattacks, you do need to know the following: when cyberattacks are successful, they can disrupt essential services and infrastructure, including transportation, water, electricity, law enforcement, and healthcare.

This begs the question: Why are governments always top of mind for cybercriminals looking to make a quick buck. When a cyberattack on a city is successful, the payday for the malicious actors involved is oftentimes substantial. For example, in June 2019, the City of Riviera Beach, located in Florida, agreed to pay $600,000 in ransom to cybercriminals who seized the city's computer systems, according to an article published by the Associated Press. While paying the ransom is not in the victim's best interest, sometimes hackers get lucky, and that is the exact reason why they continue to target governments more so than other entities.

Even though cybercriminals attack businesses of all sizes, researchers at Barracuda Networks, a provider of security, application delivery and data protection solutions, in August 2019 revealed that government organizations are the intended victims of nearly two-thirds of all ransomware attack. That statistic should worry government officials at all levels. It means cybercriminals are looking to accomplish two goals when attacking governments: a big payday and create chaos.

When IT infrastructures are not properly secured, malicious actors take advantage by exploiting system vulnerabilities, and this leaves not only our businesses in danger but also our cities.

IT infrastructures are not secured properly

What we have learned from the COVID-19 outbreak is many IT infrastructures still need to be properly secured. To accommodate the speed at which businesses needed to transition their workforces remotely, MSPs and other IT professionals acted hastily in many instances, which probably exposed some customers to cybercriminals. When working from home, employees typically are not properly protected from the increasingly complex cybersecurity threat landscape. 45 percent of employees have malware on their home networks; however, only 13.3 percent of their employers have malware on their corporate networks, according to a BitSight study published in April 2020.

The crisis also put cybersecurity issues in the spotlight when the National Governors Association called on congressional leaders to provide funding to state and local governments to address cybersecurity and IT infrastructure needs resulting from the COVID-19 outbreak. "COVID-19 has required our workforces, educational systems and general way of life to quickly move remotely, exerting greater pressure on cybersecurity and IT professionals and increasing the risk of vulnerabilities and gaps to state and local networks," the letter stated. "These gaps are exacerbated by systems requiring modernization that do not foster remote work, which also increases the risks to employees supporting these systems." Despite their ongoing challenges with foreign malicious actors, MSPs are in a better position than other businesses to assist governments with modernizing their IT infrastructures.

Some threat actors attacked specific industries during the COVID-19 crisis. For example, in May 2020, CNBC reporter Daniel Bukszpan covered a story about cybercriminals attacking pharmaceutical companies. For instance, ExecuPharm, a pharma company based in King of Prussia, Pennsylvania, experienced a data security incident (ransomware attack) in March 2020. Much of what was held for ransom during the incident were personnel files, which included employee social security numbers, passport numbers, bank account numbers, etc., according to a memo released by the State's Attorney's office. The concern over privacy was an obvious point made by many security professionals, but what many people didn't consider at the time was how the attacks could potentially interfere with the development of a COVID-19 vaccine. Would malicious actors attempt to steal data related to COVID-19 vaccines and treatments from US-based pharmaceutical companies and research institutions?

The FBI and CISA in mid-May 2020 issued a public service announcement about the possibility of one foreign power in particular targeting healthcare, pharmaceutical, and research sectors working on COVID-19 response—China. "China's efforts to target these sectors pose a significant threat to our nation's response to COVID-19," the alert stated. "This announcement is intended to raise awareness for research institutions and the American public and provide resources and guidance for those who may be targeted." Even though their work collectively is necessary in the overarching fight against the growing number of cybersecurity threats worldwide, government agencies—no matter how effective they are at what they do—cannot be the only actors defending our country from malicious threats near and far. We as a nation must also step up by doing what we can to ensure our communities are properly protected. The bad news for us is cybersecurity professionals expect the state of cybersecurity to unfortunately worsen in a post-COVID-19 world.

The numbers on how COVID-19 impacted cybersecurity efforts in the country are staggering. For example, 94 percent of cybersecurity professionals at companies with more than 100 employees were more concerned about security during the COVID-19 pandemic than before it, according to a May 2020 report published by global cybersecurity solutions provider Tripwire. The good news for them—and the American people—is 70 percent of organizations plan to increase cybersecurity spending due to the impact of the coronavirus pandemic, a May 2020 LearnBonds study reported.

Of course, MSPs are expected to benefit greatly from this change if they themselves take the proper precautions, but this is important: when I mentioned earlier that malicious actors are targeting businesses across all industries and winning—I meant it.

Are MSPs vulnerable to cyberattacks?

There is a downside to being on the frontlines; remember when medical workers lacked personal protective equipment during the COVID-19 pandemic? Unlike the average business, an MSP has access to a large amount of data, something cybercriminals always keep top of mind when monitoring potential targets for their attacks. The ASCII Group says that its average member (an MSP) has approximately 75-100 individual client businesses and is in charge of all their clients' data. Without a doubt, these malicious actors, many of whom are, quite frankly, hell-bent on finding their next big scores, are certainly aware of the networks and systems MSPs have access to on a daily basis, which is why the federal government has been alerting MSPs since 2018 about how cybercriminals are turning their attention to those committed to protecting businesses from ever-changing IT threat landscape.

CISA in October 2019 published an alert on APT actors exploiting MSPs. "Since May 2016, APT actors have used various tactics, techniques, and procedures (TTPs) for the purposes of cyber espionage and intellectual property theft," according to the alert. "APT actors have targeted victims in several US critical infrastructure sectors, including IT, energy, healthcare and public health, communications, and critical manufacturing." It was unfortunately only after CISA issued this notice that MSPs started paying closer attention to the growing number of threat actors targeting them for their unfettered access to customer networks.

Months later, in March 2019, CISA warned the business community about working with third-party companies when moving IT infrastructure to the cloud. "Since October 2018, the Cybersecurity and Infrastructure Security Agency (CISA) has conducted several engagements with customers who have used third-party partners to migrate their email services to O365," according to the alert. "The organizations that used a third party have had a mix of configurations that lowered their overall security posture (e.g., mailbox auditing disabled, unified audit log disabled, multi-factor authentication disabled on admin accounts). In addition, the majority of these organizations did not have a dedicated IT security team to focus on their security in the cloud.

These security oversights have led to user and mailbox compromises and vulnerabilities." These justified concerns tarnished the reputation of MSPs at the time of these revelations. Later that summer, these attacks, in some cases launched by foreign-state actors or intelligence agencies, capitalized on the security vulnerabilities identified at that time. Even the US Secret Service has warned the MSP community about malicious actors targeting them. The agency in a June 2020 security alert said its investigations team (GIOC—Global Investigations Operations Center) has been monitoring the actions of cybercriminals and found that there has been an increasing number of cyberattacks on MSPs.

Despite repeated warnings by their government's top cybersecurity agency, some MSPs still fell victim to hackers. Cybercriminals working with China's Ministry of State Security broke into several major MSPs, including Fujitsu, Tata Consultancy Services, NTT Data, Dimension Data, Computer Sciences Corporation and DXC Technology, in an attempt to steal commercial secrets from the MSPs' clients, according to a Reuters report published in June 2019. As expected by many, the Chinese government denied any involvement in these attacks.

Previously pointed out, ransomware attacks are a growing concern for not only businesses but also MSPs. For example, global IT consulting firm and MSP Cognizant in April 2020 confirmed it was hit by a Maze ransomware attack, which is where the attacker threatens to release the data being held publicly if the victim refuses to pay the ransom requested. "We responded quickly to investigate and remediate the attack," the company said in May 2020. "We are using this experience as an opportunity to refresh and strengthen our approach to security. We are already applying what we have learned to further harden and strengthen our security environment." Even though many of them specialize in the field of cybersecurity, MSPs make mistakes, and they are going to continue to blunder whether we consumers like it or not.

MSPs are made up of people. No matter how much they prepare and train, humans make mistakes. I cannot stress this enough: I am not making excuses for MSPs (many of them do need to do a better job of protecting themselves and their customers; the evidence is clear). I am simply stating a fact of life. Professionals err from time to time, including police officers, financial advisors, firefighters, teachers, and— even though we do not like to think about it much—doctors.

Don't forget: there is a reason why doctors pay for malpractice insurance; they, too, make mistakes occasionally. More than 250,000 people in the US die every year from medical errors (not necessarily only by doctors, themselves), according to a 2016 Johns Hopkins study. While professionals—including the ones at the top of their fields—are prone to making errors when delivering their services, we still need them to advise us on subjects we are not experts in.

Conclusion

When a crisis hits, we turn to them, the MSP specialists, despite their flaws; they can protect us from the constantly evolving threat landscape we are up against daily, and without them, these frontline workers, we cannot continue to operate our businesses without the fear of malicious actors scheming behind the scenes to take what we have from us—our livelihoods.

You may not always trust your doctors, but when there is an emergency, you put your faith in them, their expertise and the people they surround themselves with—think about the nurses, for instance. At some point, even though you may not want to, you seek the advice of a doctor when there's something wrong, and the more you learn about what they do and how they can help you, you begin to quickly realize the importance of having someone who is aware of your medical history and how you specifically can be helped.

The personal touch is what matters.

Just like with your doctor, you establish a unique personal relationship with your MSP. Your MSP understands your business, industry, systems and networks, business goals, customers, etc. You do not just call your MSP when there is an issue with your technology. Your MSP is constantly looking out for you, your employees and your customers by searching for opportunities to increase productivity and grow revenue, and implementing preventative measures to protect your business from an increasingly complex world.

The time for you to act is today.

MSPs are ready and willing to care for you if you would just let them. They should understand the hurdles you are facing and want to be by your side to guide you along the way with their expertise. There is no reason to be fearful of MSPs; look at them as potential partners.

You now know what MSPs can do for your business. They take the fear out of technology, so you can sleep at night. No big-name IT vendor, no insurance company, no telecom major carrier can protect your largest asset from an unintentional or intentional attack or outage. Only your local MSP can. That is the science of IT in the cloud and the internet era we all live in today.

You are now ready to do what it takes to operate a business in this century or advise the owner or your superior on our twenty-first century's new IT infrastructure and the vital and crucial role of the MSP. Everything you need to know about MSPs and how they can help you is now out in the open, and it is now up to you to decide whether you want to risk the health of your organization's future by ignoring symptoms and avoiding expert help, or schedule a consultation with a local MSP to prevent future complications from occurring and treating symptoms when they arise.

If you do not keep up to date with current technology and innovation, and if you do not take the effort to get to know how your particular system (be it your body or your business) is working, then your health or your network is no better than what you get from "Dr. Google."

ACKNOWLEDGMENTS

My sincere thanks go to the many hundreds of ASCII members I have personally known over the years located in all our major cities and rural towns throughout North America. I will give a specific shout out to ASCII members who helped with this book. A very special thank you to Joshua Liberman, President of Net Sciences, Inc., Albuquerque, NM, a brilliant friend, and a long-time ASCII member who read the entire manuscript to make sure all technical assertions and analysis were not just technically accurate but were a best practice in the field as tested by his peers. Additionally, Joe Balsarotti, an industry expert of long standing from St. Louis, MO area, gave special insights and cogently reviewed the manuscript carefully as a long-time member of ASCII (over 30 years) as did Jason McNew, Senior Engineer, CISSP, Appalachia Technologies, Harrisburg, PA, former Project Manager for the White House Communications Agency.

Over the years, many hundreds of ASCII corporate staff and interns helped drive our message to the industry about the key importance of the MSPs; too many to mention, so I will mention our two staff members who have been here the longest: Jerry Koutavas, our President, who along with Doug Young, our Sr. VP and COO, are two of the finest gentlemen I am lucky to know as very good friends and work day to day with, both for over 20 years. In addition, I must thank Alysia Vetter, our VP of Marketing, who helped germinate the idea for the book.

Of course, with world class experience, one could not find better speakers and educators at our events in the area of cyber security. Our two writers of the Foreword to this book we owe a real debt of gratitude: Theresa M. Payton and Frank W. Abagnale.

A very special thank you to Dr. Joshua S. Yamamoto, MD, FACC a special person in my life, who is a well-recognized Cardiologist who carefully read the entire book to affirm my thesis and with a careful, doctor's eye, and years of experience, corrected my language that may not be medically on point. If you read one medical book this year, read his recent book, "You Can Prevent a Stroke" which he coauthored with his wife, Kristin E. Thomas, MD. My brother, Daniel R. Weinberger, MD, a leading Geneticist and research doctor with years of experience who is CEO of the Lieber Institute for Brain Development, also kindly read the manuscript to make sure I am medically accurate. Brotherly love is a special love. Of course, my wife, Lauren, had very creative and helpful comments as she always does, to most anything I put my mind to do.

Finally, my helper in this writing, CJ Arlotta who did the lion's share of the research and substantial writing using my ideas and concepts to sharpen the message which hopefully will make clearer how important the local MSPs are for businesses, infrastructure, and our society as a whole.

www.ingramcontent.com/pod-product-compliance
Lightning Source LLC
Chambersburg PA
CBHW070858070326
40690CB00009B/1898